Original title:
The Answer to Life Is... Still Pending

Copyright © 2025 Creative Arts Management OÜ
All rights reserved.

Author: Henry Beaumont
ISBN HARDBACK: 978-1-80566-276-1
ISBN PAPERBACK: 978-1-80566-571-7

The Elusive Nature of Knowing

In a world of questions wide,
We search with furrowed brow,
For wisdom hidden, cleverly,
Like socks that hide somehow.

Philosophers scratching heads,
While cats chase their own tails,
They ponder complex riddles,
Like why do we have mail fails?

The meaning dances on the edge,
Like ice cream on a cone,
Just when we think we have it grasped,
It melts, leaves us alone.

A quest for truth, a merry chase,
Like finding keys misplaced,
Yet laughter echoes through the strife,
In absurdity, we find our grace.

In Pursuit of Elusive Clarity

I asked the sage a question,
But all he did was laugh.
He scribbled notes on napkins,
Then swiftly took his half.

With maps of stars and puns,
He danced around the truth.
My search for golden wisdom,
Is met with wise-guy sleuth.

The Pursuit of the Unattainable

I chased a butterfly once,
It vanished in thin air.
I pondered life's big riddles,
While hiding from despair.

A donut in my grasp,
Just out of reach again.
I guess I'm more of a sprinter,
In this marathon of Zen.

Lost in a Sea of Queries

Floating on a boat of thoughts,
With waves of 'what ifs' swell.
The fish of doubt are laughing,
They know this tale too well.

I cast a line for answers,
But all I've snagged are whines.
Each ripple, a new question,
In these comedic times.

The Spiral of Questions

Round and round I go again,
In circles, quite absurd.
While fortune cookies giggle,
Their secrets remain blurred.

Should I wear socks with sandals?
Or keep them in a drawer?
Each query spins a spiral,
I lose track; it's a chore.

The Quest for Ever-Blurred Answers.

In a world of silly signs,
We ask the stars for clues,
But they just blink and giggle,
And leave us with a snooze.

Pondering why socks go missing,
Is it a black hole's tease?
If only they'd write a note,
To say they're off to freeze.

Philosophers scratch their heads,
While the clock ticks with glee,
Searching for deep truths,
In last night's mystery brie.

With questions swirling like confetti,
We dance on floors of doubt,
Laughing at the riddles,
That life throws all about.

Eternal Questions

Why does toast always land down,
When you hope for it to fly?
Eternal questions linger,
Beneath the baffled sky.

Do cats plot our demise,
Or simply lounge with grace?
Each day is filled with wonders,
That make us laugh and race.

Is it really just a phase,
Or is that just absurd?
We ride the whims of fate,
As jokes go unheard.

With minds that twist and turn,
We play a clever game,
Collecting all the questions,
While laughing 'til we're tame.

In Search of Unseen Truths

With magnifying glasses,
We hunt for hidden laughs,
Searching every corner,
Of our chaotic paths.

Every answer seems to hide,
Behind a clever grin,
Making fools of wise men,
While the circus spins.

We question forks and knives,
Why do they always fight?
But then we trip on answers,
In the middle of the night.

The hunt goes on forever,
For truths that play coy,
If wisdom wears a tutu,
Do we laugh or say 'Oh boy'?

Awaiting Clarity in Shadows

Shadows chase with silly forms,
As we wait for them to speak,
Yet all they do is dance around,
Leaving us feeling weak.

Is coffee the secret key,
To unlock the final door?
Or is it just a potion,
To make us want more?

With fortunes written in the stars,
We expand our feeble minds,
While sipping funky cocktails,
And leaving truth behind.

So here we sit in shadows,
With chuckles and a grin,
Awaiting clarity to show,
But let the fun begin!

The Canvas of Uncertainty

A blank slate smiles back at me,
Colors of chaos dance so free.
Questions linger in the air,
While I scribble with no care.

Paint drips down the edges wide,
Each stroke a laugh, a wobbly ride.
A little chaos in the plot,
Maybe that's all I really want.

Shapes emerge but none make sense,
My brush is wild and quite intense.
It's not a mess, it's just a start,
Creating joy is quite the art.

Here in this frame of wild delight,
No answers yet, but that's all right.
I'll fill this canvas with my dreams,
And laugh at life's absurd extremes.

Holding Space for What's Yet to Be

In the waiting room of fate,
I lounge and dream about my state.
What's around the corner, oh dear?
Is it a boat? Or just a seer?

I sip my tea, I nibble scone,
The future's not here, but I'm not alone.
I chat with thoughts that pop and fizz,
Waiting for the big reveal, whiz!

A bird flies by, it gives a shrug,
"What's next?" it chirps with a playful tug.
I raise my cup, to toast the unknown,
Keep your mind light, let humor be sown.

So here's to space that's yet to come,
With giggles mingling, oh so fun.
We'll laugh and dance through mystery's door,
For life's a game, and I want more!

The Ineffable Journey

Packed my bags for the grand unknown,
With mismatched socks and a rubber bone.
Maps are good—though mine's from '89,
    Guess I'll be lost and feel just fine.

With snacks in tow and a smile quite wide,
    I hop on board for this wobbly ride.
The signs are goofy, the routes are bright,
    Every wrong turn feels just right.

Clouds look like cats, and stars are friends,
    They wink and giggle at all the bends.
    In the chaos, I find my glee,
Adventure calls, come dance with me!

As I journey through this twisted fate,
    I find humor in every state.
    In the vastness, I find my song,
What matters most is just to belong.

Beneath the Weight of Wonder

Wonder bounces like a beach ball,
Tossed around, it's fun for all.
Questions juggle, answers flee,
Beneath the weight, capriciously free.

I ponder deep while standing still,
Looking for giggles under the hill.
Is it a dragon or a fluffy cat?
Maybe it's nothing—imagine that!

The sky chuckles, clouds take flight,
"Is there a reason?" I ask the night.
With twinkling stars that wink and tease,
Life's a puzzle with missing keys.

But here I stand with awe in heart,
Each little wonder a priceless art.
So let's embrace the quirky scene,
For laughter hides in what's unseen!

Beyond the Veil of Knowing

In the land of thought we roam,
Chasing shadows, far from home.
Questions tumble, roll and spin,
While our minds wear a cheeky grin.

Wisdom dangles, just out of reach,
Like a teacher who won't teach.
Conundrums dance a merry jig,
As we ponder life's silly gig.

Clocks tick on, we scratch our heads,
Like lost sheep in tangled threads.
Each 'why' leads us to a 'who',
Tickling our brains, who knew?

So let's laugh at the absurd
And cherish each nonsensical word.
In the realm of what we don't know,
The jesters reign with a humorous glow.

The Spectrum of Wonder

Colors swirl in the mind's great maze,
Chasing thoughts in a silly haze.
With each hue comes a curvy twist,
In our quest for that cheeky list.

Laughter bubbles, theories collide,
Frustrated, yet we can't hide.
Consider frogs in tiny boats,
Who ponder life in funny quotes.

Questions should wear a playful hat,
As we scratch our heads, imagine that.
A world where answers wear a mask,
And wisdom likes to play the clown's task.

We trade our woes for silly grins,
While the universe just spins and spins.
Every ponder leads us to cheer,
For the fun lies in the questions we hear.

An Odyssey of the Unknown

In a spaceship made of dreams we fly,
Past the moons made of cheese up high.
Each star twinkles like a giggle bright,
Leading us on with mischievous delight.

Maps are scattered, the paths mislaid,
In the cosmic parade that we've made.
Are we pioneers or a comical crew?
Charting the madness as we drive through.

With telescopes made of wishful hopes,
We catch glimpses of celestial scopes.
The universe winks, an inside joke,
As we adjust our tinfoil cloak.

With each new blunder, a laugh takes flight,
An odyssey lit by humor's light.
In the vastness of what lies ahead,
May silliness guide where we dare tread.

Wading through Unclear Waters

In puddles deep of murky thought,
We splash around, tangled and caught.
Rubber ducks float, chuckling along,
While we giggle at the accidental wrong.

Navigating waves that twist and turn,
With each splash, a lesson to learn.
What's under the surface? Who knows?
Mysteries frolic like a river that glows.

Fish wear glasses, perhaps for the view,
While we ponder if they wonder too.
Life's a whirlpool of curious quests,
And humor's the sun, guiding our jest.

So let's not fret in this cloudy sea,
For the unknown holds joy, you see.
Each wave that pulls us makes us grin,
As we wade through the unclear akin.

Searching for a Flicker in the Void

In the depths of my mind, I wrack my brain,
Chasing shadows like thoughts on a train.
With each funny thought, the moment I smile,
Where's the logic in this? Just wait a while.

I ponder the stars, are they just a jest?
Or do they twinkle because of a test?
If wisdom's a riddle, I'm lost in the game,
But perhaps it's the search that's bringing the fame.

Awaiting the Dawn of Understanding

Tick-tock goes the clock, what's on the shelf?
Answers are hiding, even from myself.
I greet every morning with coffee and dreams,
Hoping to uncover those elusive themes.

Like socks in the dryer, where do they go?
The mysteries linger, but none seem to show.
As the sun rises up with a grin on its face,
I laugh at the puzzle — it's quite the race!

The Palette of Possible Realities

Colors of chaos swirl in my mind,
Creating a picture that's wonderfully blind.
With brushes of nonsense, I paint and I play,
Who knew confusion could brighten the day?

Each hue represents a thought that I chase,
Some tickle my fancy, while others embrace.
In the gallery of life, absurd art reigns clear,
I mime, laugh, and giggle, no need for a seer.

Time: A Blank Scroll

A blank sheet of time, it lies by my side,
Waiting for scribbles of things I can't hide.
As I doodle and dash, the ink's running free,
What wisdom will spill? It's anyone's spree!

In the margins, I sketch out my hopes and my fears,
With a wink and a nod, I'll laugh through the years.
So here's to the chaos, the fun, and the twist,
Life's but a joke, and I love the absurdist!

Still Searching for the Key

In pockets deep, I rummage through,
Have I checked the left, or the right shoe?
Keys to puzzles dance and tease,
Might they be hidden in a box of cheese?

I ask my cat, she just yawns wide,
She seems content, no need to hide.
I'm sure it's here, just lost for good,
Maybe it's stuck in the neighborhood wood.

A squirrel winks, as if he knows,
Yet all he does is steal my clothes.
The key to life or just my door?
Is it a riddle? I need a score!

So here I sit, with tea in hand,
Pondering mysteries, oh so grand.
If I find it, will I laugh or cry?
Maybe I'll just wave it goodbye!

Windswept on the Path to Truth

With hair askew and thoughts in flight,
I chase the wisps that feel so right.
Truth has a way of playing coy,
Like a child's toy that brings pure joy.

Do I walk left, or take the right?
The wind just giggles, out of sight.
I slip on clouds, a cotton fluff,
Is this the truth, or just enough?

In dandelion fields, I spin and whirl,
Each seed a thought, each twirl a swirl.
Do I know more now? Oh, who can say,
I might just nap instead, hooray!

Still I wander, amongst the breeze,
Just one more question, if you please.
Is there a map, or a guidebook here?
The laughter of leaves is all I hear.

As Time Drifts Away

Tick-tock, the clock makes its sound,
Yet answers hide, never to be found.
I wave at seconds as they fly,
"Come back!" I shout, but they just sigh.

A loaf of bread, and tea for two,
Are we closer to knowledge? Not a clue.
As minutes slip like sand from hands,
I search for meaning in these bands.

So here I sit, with crumbs and cheer,
Contemplating all that I hold dear.
If time is a friend, why is it naught?
Maybe it's busy, lost in thought.

And as I ponder, the sun goes down,
My wisdom fades, a sleepy frown.
So I'll just dream of futures bright,
Maybe tomorrow I'll get it right!

The Potential of Unimagined Futures

Imagine a world made of ice cream,
Where work is a game and life's a dream.
We'd float on clouds, and dive in pie,
With sprinkles of laughter, oh me, oh my!

Would unicorns roam, or issues persist?
Maybe we need more than we've missed.
A horizon blooms with colors unspun,
Yet here I am, just aiming for fun.

What if we danced with shadows at night,
Made jokes with the stars, oh what a sight!
Would wisdom come wrapped in silly hats?
Or found in the tales of chatting cats?

The future is a dance, a comic groove,
Where joy is the step, and laughter moves.
So let's spin ahead, with hearts aglow,
Because who needs answers, just let it flow!

Existence in a Limbo

Caught in a loop, we dance and sway,
Chasing our tails on this wobbly bay.
With cosmic jokes that never land,
We giggle and grin, but don't understand.

Why do socks vanish in the wash?
Is there a truth we simply posh?
The cat knows more, we think he's wise,
With his judgmental yet sleepy eyes.

Pizza or salad, that's our deep quest,
But all we find is a hungry jest.
For every answer, a riddle grows,
And laughter erupts, where curiosity flows.

So we twirl in confusion, hands up to the sky,
With a pie in our face, I ask, "Oh my!"
In this limbo of life, let's toast with a cheer,
To all the oddities we hold so dear.

Unraveled Questions

Why is the toaster such a tease,
Always leaves crumbs, like it's trying to please?
As we ponder our fate over buttered bread,
The mysteries of life swirl round in our head.

Is cereal a soup? Let's shout it aloud,
With unconventional flavors, we'd gather a crowd.
Among random wonders, we laugh and we joke,
In this grand inquiry, we're all just a poke.

Who decided that grass should be green?
Or that washing dishes is rarely routine?
Each query unravels, like pasta untwined,
Swirling in chaos, no sense to find.

But amidst our confusion, we wear silly hats,
Playing the fool with all our chats.
In a world full of questions, let's skedaddle and play,
For laughter's the answer, come what may.

Whispers of Uncertainty

In the realm of the absurd, we frolic and spin,
Whispers of doubt keep the fun rolling in.
With a wiggle and jiggle, we sidestep the gloom,
Sipping on smiles like flowers that bloom.

What's the deal with the garden gnome?
Staring at weeds, he feels like home.
We debate our existence while eating some pie,
Just trying to figure out the "whys" and the "hi's."

Jumping at shadows, we laugh at the chase,
Like a squirrel in a tree, finding nutty embrace.
As echoes of reasoning flutter and fade,
We wrap up our thoughts in a cozy charade.

So here's to the riddles and silly old quirks,
With each nutty pondering, the laughter just works.
In whispers of uncertainty, let's raise a toast,
To the humorous chaos we love the most.

The Clock Ticks Unanswered

Tick-tock goes the clock, in a funny debate,
While we wonder and wander, it won't seal our fate.
Count all the seconds, they slide and they swoosh,
Until we find answers, or simply a whoosh.

Time's a tricky thing, it winks and it blinks,
Perplexing our thoughts, making us rethink.
Is time really linear, or just a grand jest?
As we bumble and fumble, we try our best.

Between the minutes, the grins and the laughs,
We juggle our worries like comical gaffes.
As the hands on the dial spin wildly around,
We dive into absurdity, so blissfully unbound.

So let's cherish the moments, each tick from the clock,
With a wink and a smile, we'll take it as stock.
For when life hands questions, we're game for the ride,
In this wacky parade, we'll laugh-cry with pride.

Unwritten Pages of Existence

In the book of life, we scribble and doodle,
Searching for wisdom, like finding a poodle.
With sticky notes here and a pen that won't write,
We laugh at our questions that dance in the light.

The coffee is strong, as we ponder the day,
While socks in the dryer have gone far away.
We joke about aliens and taxes in spring,
Wondering what all of this nonsense could bring.

We spin like a top, searching answers in air,
Creating a circus with flair and with care.
Perhaps in the chaos, a clue might just pop,
To tell us the secret of this crazy hop.

In margins and gaps, hope's scribbled in blue,
A punchline awaits, it's just missing its cue.
We'll laugh till we cry, then we'll giggle some more,
As life's unwritten pages keep opening doors.

A Quest for Meaning

In a world full of questions, we set out to roam,
With backpacks of wonder, we leave our warm home.
Each street corner whispers a riddle, a jest,
And we chase down the giggles, avoiding the rest.

The meaning of life is like socks in the wash,
They vanish like magic, then suddenly, posh!
Through stores labeled 'serious' and cafes that sigh,
We search for a glimpse, while we munch on a pie.

With each twist and turn, we find chuckles and sighs,
Why is that owl wearing clear plastic disguise?
The books seem to smile, the clouds give a wink,
As we ponder the big questions while barely a blink.

The journey's quite wacky, yet here we all stand,
Sharing tales with the moon and the sun's golden hand.
Perhaps in the laughter, we'll stumble on tracks,
That lead to the punchline or a group of wise quacks.

Echoes of Uncertainty

Amidst the loud echoes of canines that bark,
We ponder our purpose from dawn until dark.
With spoons made of waffle, we stir up the doubt,
Sipping on dreams, as we wander about.

The clock ticks in riddles, the seconds all tease,
As we dance with confetti, and float like a breeze.
The ants in the grass hold debates with the sky,
While we giggle at the owls who wholeheartedly try.

With each fib of a friend, we chuckle and grin,
As cats in top hats spin tales in the din.
The universe chuckles, a cosmic confound,
In the echoes of nonsense, hilarity's found.

With joy as our compass, we sail on this sea,
Where questions abound but answers are flee.
Let's toast to the journey, pour lemonade sweet,
As we frolic in laughter, life can't be beat!

The Riddle of the Cosmos

The stars wear their glasses, the moon cracks a smile,
As we ponder the cosmos, it's quite the long mile.
Galaxies giggle in colors so bright,
While planets play hopscotch in the hush of the night.

With telescopes made of silly old dreams,
We search for the meaning in whimsical beams.
The nebula chuckles, "It's simpler than you!
Just dance in your pajamas and sing out of tune!"

A comet zooms by with a wink and a grin,
"Why worry about answers? Just twirl and spin!"
The riddle grows funnier as shadows take flight,
In this cosmic adventure, we find pure delight.

With laughter as stardust, and whimsy as fate,
We craft the absurd as we gallop through space.
Watch cosmic balloons float to the beat,
As we savor the chaos, life's humor is sweet!

The Gap Between Stars

In the cosmos, whispers roam,
Questions linger, light-years from home.
Aliens giggle, they sip on tea,
'What's the secret? Come tell us, please!'

Galaxies dance with a twinkle and tease,
While cosmic beings munch on space cheese.
Gravity plays tag, it's quite absurd,
But answers hide, not a single word.

Black holes swallow ideas whole,
Asteroids laugh, they lose control.
In this vast void, we often ponder,
Maybe truth's just a cosmic blunder!

So we float in this puzzling night,
Chasing riddles, taking flight.
With each twinkle, we burst with glee,
In this grand joke, are we the key?

Threads of a Frayed Reality

Life's fabric unravels, a tangled weave,
Mismatched patterns, can't quite believe.
Socks go missing, ties lose their place,
Stretching the truth, it's a slippery space.

Frayed ends waving, a woolly parade,
Dancing with quirks, all neatly displayed.
Reality laughs, it's wearing a grin,
While logic takes a sip from a tin.

Stitches unravel, zippers refuse,
Epiphanies wander, choose-lose or snooze?
We trip on the threads, our minds in a whirl,
Wrinkled ideas begin to unfurl.

So here we are, in this chaos divine,
Tangled together, seeking the line.
With humor intact, we take a brief pause,
In this frayed fabric, we cheer and applaud!

When Certainty Wavers

Certainty's a jester, flips a coin,
Says, 'Pick a side, but don't you join!'
We nod our heads, with a smirk and a shake,
Wondering loudly, what choice will we make?

Logic breaks down, like an old rusty bike,
Happiness is lost, gives a playful strike.
We search for anchors in a salty sea,
But the waves just chuckle, 'Who's got the key?'

Clocks tick backward, time takes a leap,
While grumpy old answers are stuck in a heap.
Doubts run rampant, on a wild spree,
We throw up our hands, 'Aren't we just free?'

In wobbly moments, we laugh and we cry,
Because who needs answers when you can ask why?
With winks and with giggles, let's ride this wave,
In the dance of uncertainty, we might just be brave!

Life's Ongoing Inquiry

What's the point of this wild charade?
Is it to laugh, or just be afraid?
Questions pop up like toast from a toaster,
Burnt on the edges, are we the poster?

We wander through life like lost little ducks,
Quacking for sense but stuck in the muck.
Philosophers ponder with furrowed brow,
While pigeons just coo, 'What's that all about?'

In the circus of thoughts, we juggle our fate,
Clowns in our heads, suggest we play straight.
Yet chaos delights in a playful spree,
Yelling, 'No structure's the way to be free!'

So let's toast to the questions, the curious blend,
Riding the waves where confusion transcends.
In laughter and joy, we'll embrace the unknown,
For in every inquiry, we've all truly grown!

Unraveled Threads of Understanding

In a room full of thinkers, we scratch our heads,
Searching for answers, lost in our beds.
We poke at the mysteries, twist and shout,
Wondering if logic is turning about.

A goldfish gives wisdom, it swims in a bowl,
Saying to me, "You've got to let go!"
With every wild theory, we laugh and spin,
Trusting the chaos of where we have been.

The cat on the mat looks so sly and keen,
Claiming the universe is just one big meme.
We gather our snacks, let the questions flow,
Expecting epiphanies, but not really though.

So here we are thinking, with smiles that gleam,
Fueled by confusion, each thought a theme.
With humor as our guide, we dance and we jest,
In the grand game of guessing, we're all quite blessed.

A Journey Beyond the Stars

We packed our odd theories in rockets so bright,
Zooming past planets, oh what a sight!
The stars winked at us with a twinkling glee,
While we plotted our course to the cosmic tea.

A sentient cloud said, 'You're really quite daft,
Seeking great wisdom in this interstellar craft.'
We laughed at the cosmos, drank stars like wine,
Toasting to nonsense, our spirits entwined.

Orbiting thoughts that just seemed to float,
Bouncing on comets, in our noodle boat.
We scribbled equations on stardusty sand,
But the answers eluded, like grains slipping hand.

With every bright flash, our giggles grew loud,
Who knew that confusion could form such a cloud?
So off we keep sailing on this cosmic spree,
Finding joy in the questions, that's how it should be.

The Loom of Possibility

Weaving our dreams on a curious loom,
Threads of confusion, creating a room.
Patterns of nonsense twirl through the air,
Each stitch an enigma we giggle and share.

The fabric of thought seems to tangle and twist,
Yet somehow it forms a bright patchwork mist.
With each little knot, we unravel the fear,
And laugh at the logic just vanishing here.

Our loom spins a tale of ridiculous fun,
Dancing in circles until we are spun.
While searching for meaning, we trip and we fall,
Finding delight in the questions of all.

So grab a bright thread, let's stitch up our minds,
Together in chaos, what joy that it finds!
We're lost in the fabric where uncertainties dwell,
But isn't it funny? We're not doing too well!

Navigating the Unknown

With a compass of giggles, we set forth tonight,
Charting the uncharted, oh what a delight!
Our map is a doodle, a whimsical maze,
Each turn brings a chuckle, each path a craze.

The wilderness sings with a curious tone,
We're lost but not lonely, together we've grown.
Uncharted dimensions keep giving us clues,
In the land of the puzzled, we've nothing to lose.

Our GPS is a cat, it's guiding us through,
Meowing directions to enlighten our crew.
While stumbling on riddles that tickle our brains,
We laugh through the puzzles, ignoring the pains.

So onward we journey, absurdity reigns,
Each question a journey that joyously gains.
And though we may wander, now, isn't it clear?
The fun's not in answers, but in laughing, my dear!

In the Silence of Anticipation

A riddle wrapped in a joke,
As I ponder and choke,
My coffee's getting cold,
Where's the wisdom I'm sold?

I asked a wise old cat,
"Hey, what's up with that?"
He stretched and then yawned,
"Dude, I'm honestly pawnd."

With each tick of the clock,
I'm plotting a mock,
Perhaps I'll find the clue,
In last week's gumshoe.

So here I am in thought,
With questions I've naught,
Balancing life's great jest,
Maybe just give it rest.

The Art of Uncertainty

Standing in line for my fate,
Is it chance or just fate?
The lottery of the unknown,
Toss me a text on my phone.

With every choice I make,
I wonder if I'll break,
Like a piñata in a game,
Will I find fortune or blame?

I flip a coin for a sign,
Heads or tails, it's quite fine,
But it bounces off my shoe,
Saying nothing, just boo-hoo.

In the classroom of life,
Where confusion is rife,
I laugh, I shrug, I sigh,
Maybe the truth's just a lie.

The Mirror of the Unfathomable

I peered into the glass,
What a curious mass,
Reflections of confusion,
Endless thoughts, a fusion.

The mirror grinned at me,
A trick, or could it be?
Its surface cracked with wit,
No answers, just a split.

I asked it for advice,
A charm or some spice,
It whispered back with glee,
"Just live, and then you'll see!"

So I danced with my doubts,
Filling in all the routes,
In the shimmer of the night,
I chuckled at my plight.

Glimpses of Tomorrow's Answers

Peeking at the future's door,
Oh, what lies in store?
A calendar with no dates,
Just dancing with our fates.

Tomorrow plans a party,
But the invite's tardy,
We scribble on the walls,
Collecting life's miscalls.

I sought a wise old sage,
"Help me turn the page,"
He laughed and threw confetti,
Said, "Chill, things get messy!"

So here I stake my claim,
With humor as my game,
For when life's a circus show,
Just juggle the woes and flow.

Navigating the Unknown

Maps are scribbles, wild and bright,
I steer my ship through day and night.
The compass spins, a dance unplanned,
Lost with a smile, I wave my hand.

The stars above just wink in jest,
"Adventure's calling, take your rest."
I jot my thoughts on napkins torn,
While pondering fate, I'm only worn.

Each twist we make, a laughter's cheer,
A crook in life, it ends up clear.
We roam the shores where the wild things play,
And chuckle at clouds that block the way.

Footprints on Shifting Sands

With every step, the ground gives way,
I chase my thoughts like a child at play.
The footprints fade in a sly retreat,
And tease my hopes with sandy heat.

Seagulls cackle with knowing grins,
While tumbles and tumbles, my journey spins.
Each grain a giggle, each wave a sigh,
"Keep chewing gum, just don't ask why!"

The tide rolls in, my doubts get tossed,
But I'll still wade, no matter the cost.
Life's a beach, or so they say,
As I dance on sand, come what may.

Searching for Light in the Gloom

In shadows deep where giggles live,
I hunt for laughter, it's what I give.
Flashlights flicker and jokes collide,
While monsters under beds just hide.

A cheshire cat in a foggy trance,
He grins and grins, inviting dance.
I stumble on, with toes in plight,
Yet somehow, still, I find my light.

A riddle here, a pun in tow,
In laughter's glow, I finally glow.
With every snicker, the gloom departs,
As joy keeps beating in hopeful hearts.

The Unsung Tapestry of Existence

Threads of humor woven tight,
In life's grand fabric, oh what a sight!
Each burst of laughter, a stitch so bold,
Creating stories that never get old.

Some knots are tricky, some threads go slack,
Yet pulling them tight, I can't look back.
The colors clash, but that's the fun,
In this crazy quilt, we're never done.

Each patch, a moment, absurd and rare,
With patterns of joy showing we care.
Life's tapestry is hand-sewn with grace,
And laughter's the thread that we all embrace.

Beneath the Surface of Certainty

Beneath the waves of what we know,
Fish swim in circles, putting on a show.
With hats and shoes, they strut around,
Unaware of truths that can't be found.

In bubbles of logic, they puff with pride,
Chasing their tails, in circles they glide.
Each splash of wisdom is a jester's joke,
While seashells giggle, the currents choke.

The Dance of Possibilities

Around the ballroom, doubts do sway,
With wiggle and twirl, they lead the way.
A two-step stumble, a cha-cha chase,
Possibilities glide in a comical race.

Even the walls wear a curious grin,
As paradoxes boogie and toss out the pin.
Laughter echoes as logic trips,
On the dance floor of whims, the reason skips.

Between Questions and Stars

High in the sky, a question takes flight,
Hovering, wondering, through the night.
Stars chuckle softly, winks in their glow,
What answers lie hidden, they just don't know.

With a flicker of light, and a twinkle of flair,
Questions pirouette in the cool midnight air.
In constellations, mysteries do parley,
While comets pass by, laughing all the way.

The Labyrinth of the Mind

In the maze of thoughts, no exit in sight,
A hamster wheel spins, its frantic delight.
With signs pointing nowhere, confusion reigns,
While echoes of wisdom slip down the drains.

Lost in the corridors of what's up and down,
Where whirlwinds of notions wear reason's frown.
A jester lurks round each tangled bend,
Shouting, 'Keep looking, the fun never ends!'

Puzzles in the Cosmos

Stars spin tales we can't untangle,
Galaxies giggle, their secrets dangle.
Black holes chuckle at our lost socks,
While comets play hopscotch on orbiting rocks.

Aliens ponder in spaceships so bright,
Laughing at humans all day and night.
With signs we can't read and puzzles unsolved,
We ponder our fate as we're thrown and revolved.

Each question a riddle, each answer a quest,
Like a cat chasing shadows, we rarely find rest.
The universe twirls with a wink and a tease,
While we search for meaning like kids on the breeze.

Perhaps it's a game with a twist and some fun,
Where the fun's in the chase, not the finish we run.
So here's to the laughter and fumbles we make,
In the cosmic circus, let's dance for our sake.

The Great Dilemma's Dance

Two paths diverge, and both look appealing,
One's filled with pizza, the other's a ceiling.
Should I take the plunge or stay on the shore?
My mind is a tango, my heart wants to roar.

Should I choose the path where the donuts are round,
Or follow the trail that leads underground?
Each step is a giggle, each choice a delight,
When life throws confetti, just hold on tight.

Do I jump to the left or shimmy to the right?
The universe chuckles, savvy and bright.
Round and round we go, a merry-go-fun,
As dilemmas do dance, we're just here for the pun.

So grab your partners, let's swirl like a pro,
In this great dilemma, just go with the flow.
Life's a frosting-covered cake, take a slice,
Even if the outcome isn't too precise.

Between Hopes and Hesitations

Standing on the edge of a vast ocean breeze,
Wondering if I'll catch the next wave with ease.
Should I jump or just wobble, a whimsical sway?
While seagulls debate if they'll ever come play.

Dreams float on clouds, all fluffy and white,
But doubts dance like shadows, obscuring the light.
Should I chase the rainbow or just watch it from here?
While my thoughts do a dance, both shaky and clear.

Should I go for the gold or settle for fun?
Life's a big riddle that's never quite done.
Choices and chances like jellybeans spread,
Mix up your colors, go wild in your head.

In this circus of hopes, we wobble and sway,
Giggles sprinkled like sunshine each day.
With a wink to the sky, let's stumble with grace,
Navigating this dance, let's join the embrace.

A Symphony of Half-Truths

Conductors wave batons in this life's grand parade,
Where harmonies clash with a bit of charade.
Is it real or a figment, this tune we all hum?
Life's symphony plays while we tap our own drum.

Whispers of wisdom float through the air,
Like confetti at parties, they scatter everywhere.
But hidden behind them are giggles quite sly,
As we dance with dilemmas, oh me, oh my!

Here's a note made of laughter, a chord of delight,
With echoes of "maybe" that soar through the night.
So let's sing our half-truths, we'll croon like the pros,
In a world full of questions, just strike up your pose.

As the music plays on and the moments unwind,
What's true is elusive, a treasure to find.
So let's revel in laughter, let's twirl and we'll spin,
In this symphony of life, we all get to win!

Beyond Words

In the world of queries, we play,
Searching for wisdom, come what may.
Questions like bubbles float in the air,
Popping with giggles, laughter to share.

Tick-tock goes the clock, it spins,
Chasing answers through thick and thin.
But when we find them, they seem so slight,
Like socks in the dryer, lost out of sight.

Pondering big things with tiny brains,
Chasing the sun, avoiding the rains.
Ideas parade like ducks in a row,
But what's the punchline? Do we really know?

Jokes on us, we stumble and dance,
In the quest for meaning, we take a chance.
With laughs in our pockets and quirks all around,
Maybe the joy is where truth can be found.

Beyond Time

In a clockwork maze where time likes to play,
We ask questions that never decay.
Backwards and forwards, we spin like a top,
Searching for answers that never quite drop.

Years cling together like socks in a pair,
Memories slide, but do we care?
Each moment a riddle, a tick and a tock,
Like trying to pet an elusive clock.

Time drinks its coffee, then spills on the floor,
Winks at the chaos and then asks for more.
With timeless folly, we dance in the haze,
Wondering through life in a daze of days.

And when the page turns, what do we see?
A blank line waiting… for some kind of glee.
In the book of our life, we're all scribblers and clowns,
Making the best of this circus of crowns.

Caught in the Tides of Thought

Surfing on notions, we ride the waves,
Caught in the currents of whims that we crave.
Thoughts float like jellyfish, shiny and round,
Stinging and tickling, they dance all around.

With brains like sponges, we soak up the fun,
Misting our worries like rays from the sun.
But each tide that rolls in is both silly and bright,
Like trying to catch stars with a net made of light.

Wave after wave, our brains twist and whirl,
Caught in a riddle that makes our heads twirl.
But when the tide ebbs, and calm comes to play,
Do we find all the answers? Oh wait, not today!

So let's float on this sea, with laughter our guide,
Embracing the chaos, we take it in stride.
With each question we ponder, we giggle and beam,
In the ocean of nonsense, we'll follow our dream.

The Cascade of Unsung Answers

A waterfall whispers, "Come, take a peek,"
But the answers it offers are rather oblique.
They tumble and splash, oh what a surprise,
Spritzing the seekers, confusing the wise.

Questions cascade like leaves in the wind,
Crafted with humor, oh where to begin?
Each drop is a giggle, a riddle to crack,
Slipping through fingers, who'd want to go back?

The flow of confusion seems endless and bright,
In the misty mayhem, we revel in light.
As laughter flows freely, we swim with glee,
Chasing the echoes, so wild and so free.

So gather your thoughts, let the water flow on,
With each twist and turn, new questions are drawn.
In the cascade of moments, we relish the charms,
Unraveling life's puzzle, wrapped up in warm arms.

The Yet-Unwritten Chapter of Existence

Pages all blank, the pen's poised to write,
What's next in this story? Oh, it feels so light.
Each word a giggle, each line a surprise,
The plot thickens daily, oh how time flies!

Chasing the scribbles of dreams in our heads,
Trying to figure these tangled threads.
Will it be romance or just silly rhymes?
A tale of lost socks and tumble-down climes?

In this novel we craft, with humor so grand,
We dance through the chapters, hand in hand.
Flipping through moments, we giggle and sigh,
With irony sprinkled, oh my, oh my!

So let's write the story, one laugh at a time,
In the yet-unwritten, we'll find our own rhyme.
The journey is wild, let's embrace every quirk,
In the book of existence, where silliness lurks!

Echoes of an Unsung Truth

In a world of 'why' and 'how',
We dance around the sacred cow.
Pondering on the great unknown,
While internet memes have overgrown.

With each question, laughter swells,
Deep thoughts sealed in tiny shells.
Is it napping or is it fate?
We laugh as we contemplate.

Pickled wisdom in a jar,
Hoping to reach that distant star.
But I'll settle for snacks and fun,
Where answers fade, yet smiles are spun.

Chasing Shadows of Meaning

In the corner, a shadow gleams,
Waving hello, or so it seems.
We chase it down, it slips away,
Shadow games are here to stay.

Thoughts like bubbles, floating high,
Pop! And now we ask why.
Each little giggle, a puzzle piece,
As reasons dodge and never cease.

Questions spiral, like clowns on bikes,
Life's not serious—just ask the mics.
We juggle hopes and dreams, you see,
Finding joy in lunacy.

In Search of the Elusive Key

I'm hunting for that grand old key,
To unlock secrets none can see.
But every door that I pursue,
Leads to the fridge—I find my stew.

Locks and riddles, oh, what they say,
Chasing joy can feel like play.
But where's the treasure, that's the quiz,
Perhaps it's hiding in a fizz?

A map of nonsense, silly designs,
The truth lost in punchlines and signs.
So here's a toast to all the fun,
To question marks under the sun!

A Journey Without a Map

With no compass, I wander wide,
Following giggles like a guide.
Where are we headed, who can tell?
Each step's a story, cast a spell.

Paths uncertain, dancing feet,
Life's a carnival, oh, so sweet.
I'll embrace the chaos like a champ,
Here's to venturing—sans the stamp!

In every detour, laughter blooms,
Truth hides among the funny fumes.
So join me now, let's strut and swerve,
In this wild ride we all deserve!

The Silence of Certainty

In quiet rooms where thoughts do play,
The echoes bounce, then fade away.
We scribble notes on napkin dreams,
Yet all it gets is silent screams.

Majestic claims of wisdom great,
Yet still we ponder quite a rate.
With coffee cups stacked high in stacks,
We laugh at life, just cut the cracks.

The obvious sits right in our view,
A cupboard full of socks, just two!
If certainty leads, it must be lost,
In the realm of thoughts at any cost.

We chase our tails in circles neat,
Inventing truths, oh what a feat!
As laughter lifts our heavy hearts,
We dance away from all the smarts.

Footprints in the Sand of Time

Each footprint bends beneath the wave,
A tale of mischief, bold and brave.
We trudge through sands with big, loud feet,
Yet wonder where we missed the beat.

The sunbeams laugh as shadows stretch,
A riddle stands, but who will fetch?
With every step, a thousand doubts,
Yet still we dance, as life shouts out.

Our hats are filled with thoughts absurd,
Like owls that hoot but never herd.
We skip over tomorrows plight,
Holding tight to dreams in flight.

So etch your footprints, let them shine,
While giggles echo through the brine.
For in this game of sands and time,
We find our joy, our fits of rhyme.

Whispers of the Unknown

A breeze in whispers, soft and sly,
Tells stories where the shadows lie.
We chase the tales on misty nights,
And question owls with curious sights.

The unknown stirs in lumpy beds,
Where dreams conjoin and tumble heads.
Tickles from fate, a playful tease,
We tumble forth, just aim to please.

Like chasing cats who steal our socks,
We're wrapped in riddles, edgy box.
The universe winks with a sly grin,
While we fumble through, and life spins.

So gather 'round, embrace the jest,
In contradictions, we'll find our best.
For in life's play, both wild and calm,
Lies laughter's pulse, forever balm.

Pending Revelations

A clock ticks on with raucous glee,
As questions flutter, wild and free.
We scribble thoughts on bathroom tiles,
And giggle at our own green miles.

"Oh dear," we say, "what's left to know?"
As answers dart like a back row show.
With popcorn prompts, we watch in awe,
It's comedy gold with every flaw.

The lightbulbs flicker, bright then dim,
A dance of insights, oh so grim.
But laughter rings from every quest,
In pending truths, we find our zest.

So here we stand, all in a line,
Exploring layers, like fine wine.
In this circus of life, we see,
Pending revelations set us free!

An Inkwell of Unfinished Stories

Inkwells filled to the brim,
With tales that never begin.
Characters lose their way,
Their punchlines in dismay.

Scraps of humor in a pile,
Making us think, 'What's the style?'
A story starts, then makes a run,
Leaving us laughing, not quite done.

The quill's poised, but then it falls,
Echoes of laughter, just silly calls.
Chapters open, yet they stall,
Like a comedy that grips but won't enthrall.

So here we are, with ink still wet,
Waiting for the laugh we'll get.
Jokes in drafts, lost to time,
Creating punchlines in a wobbly rhyme.

Unanswered within the Echo

Whispers bounce in empty halls,
Tickled with unanswered calls.
Echoes laughing, oh what fun,
Chasing questions, on the run.

"Why's the sky blue?" we all ask,
But the answer's a hefty task.
With giggles ricocheting wide,
It hides in the turn of the tide.

Laughter echoes off the walls,
While reason quietly stalls.
In the chaos of the sound,
Answers flutter all around.

But still we walk this curious track,
With echoes always coming back.
Wrapped in humor, we drift along,
In the melody of a nonsensical song.

Threads Yet to be Woven

Threads of thought hang by a string,
Unraveled tales that never cling.
Stitching laughter into the seams,
Frayed ideas, just silly dreams.

Each loop a giggle, untied and wild,
Patchwork stories, a joke compiled.
But the fabric's a bit askew,
Colors bright but with no clue.

Crafting answers from a loom,
Fuzzy logic in the room.
Patterns shift and twist away,
Leaving us puzzled in a play.

Yet what's a meme but a wondrous thread?
It tickles the mind, plants seeds of dread.
With every stitch that's left undone,
Life's a quilt of trips and fun.

The Mystery of What Lies Ahead

Footsteps forward, all a-riddle,
Hilarity playing the fiddle.
Maps drawn with questionable ink,
Pointing to places we wouldn't think.

Fate's a jester, pulling strings,
Laughing at our wildest flings.
We wonder what's in store, you see,
If life's a joke, we're part of the spree.

With every plot twist, we just laugh,
As uncertainty carves our path.
Tomorrows tiptoe, full of surprise,
And we just giggle at our own demise.

So let's embrace the unknown grin,
Dance on the edges, let's begin.
For in the end, whatever is fed,
Life's just fun, it's all in our head.

Beneath the Surface of What Is

In a world of silly hats,
Answers hide like furry cats.
We search high, we search low,
But wisdom's always on the go.

Thoughts are swimming, quite absurd,
Like ducks who never learned a word.
We ponder deep in our tea,
What could the truth even be?

Every riddle comes with cheese,
Life's a joke with a hint of wheeze.
So let's laugh at the silly dance,
While fate spins us another chance.

Beneath the surface, truth's a prank,
Like searching for a ship that sank.
With giggles echoing from the bay,
The more we question, the less we sway.

The Unwritten Pages of Tomorrow

Tomorrow's yet to spill its ink,
Blank pages nod and tease, I think.
What rhymes with destiny unknown?
My coffee's cold, I need a loan.

Do we scribble tales of gold?
Or write about the socks we fold?
Each choice a puzzle, each step wild,
Like a toddler's dance, unrefined and mild.

In the book of life, we search and roam,
Pages flutter like a wayward gnome.
Unwritten stories crave a voice,
In the chaos, we still rejoice.

With each blank line, a chance to play,
In a wobbly world where cats lead the way.
So let's see what nonsense it brings,
In the dance of tomorrow, oh, how it swings!

Moments of Fleeting Epiphany

A flash of light, then poof, it's gone,
Like a sock that vanished at dawn.
Epiphanies are sneaky things,
They leave us wondering what joy brings.

In cereal boxes, wisdom creeps,
Amidst the crunch, that knowledge leaps.
We scribble notes on napkin trails,
While laughter dances, even fails.

Moments pass like buses late,
With every stop, we re-evaluate.
Pondering life with a side of fries,
Is this the plan? Who truly tries?

Yet in the chaos, joy will find,
The tiniest spark to unwind.
So let's embrace the silly chase,
In moments frayed, we find our place.

Harmony in the Questions

Questions pop like bubble wrap,
Each one leads to a comic mishap.
What's the meaning, why do we care?
Like a squirrel stuck up in a chair.

Chasing thoughts that buzz and zing,
In the riddle of this silly fling.
Life's a whodunit with no clue,
The plot twist? A dog in a shoe!

We laugh at what we can't explain,
While reasoning gets stuck in the rain.
Oh, what fun in the curious breeze,
As joy sings sweet from the leafy trees.

So gather round, come share your whims,
In the music of life, we dance on rims.
With harmony found in every jest,
We live the questions, and embrace the quest.

The Rhythm of Ambivalence

In a dance of yes and no,
Feet shuffle, unsure where to go.
Should I leap or take a seat?
Both paths smell of stale cheese feet.

The clock ticks, what's the next step?
Coffee's strong, but still I misrep.
I question if my socks align,
And wonder where I misdefined.

To jump or wait, what's the score?
The answers hide behind the door.
Clowns juggle life in wobbly ways,
As I toss coins in a foggy haze.

So here I spin, a topsy-turvy
In a world that feels so unaware of me.
Life's quirky tunes make no good sense,
A riddle wrapped in a silly pretense.

Truths that Linger Like Smoke

I light a fire to warm the air,
But truths emerge, all in disrepair.
Like smoke rings swirling round and round,
Such clarity is nowhere found.

I scribble notes on a paper plate,
Each thought's a joke, but feel the weight.
With every puff, I start to see,
Life's questions dance unpredictably.

Should I laugh, or might I cry?
Wisdom's shy, just passing by.
I compose a sonnet in the dark,
While my cat sneezes with a spark.

Chasing phantoms of thoughts once bold,
I trip on dreams that never sold.
Truths linger, foggy, in the air,
A ticklish riddle, forever rare.

The Palette of Perpetual Inquiry

Brush in hand, I start to paint,
A canvas filled with doubts that taint.
Is that orange or just a shade?
The colors melt, I'm feeling swayed.

Questions drip like a leaky pen,
Why don't fish wear shoes, my friend?
I'm lost in hues of deep confusion,
Amateur art is my conclusion.

Swirls of 'maybe' blush on the side,
While 'what ifs' run like a tide.
In this gallery of curious fright,
Masterpieces move, but none feel right.

Time's a brush that never dries,
Each stroke a giggle, each smile a sigh.
To color or not, that's the plight,
In this humorous haze of light.

Stars We Cannot Reach

I gaze up where the planets zoom,
Finding wishes in cosmic gloom.
Comets whip by, like fast trains,
Yet answers float like runaway chains.

Astrologers craft maps of the skies,
But I get lost, what a surprise!
The Great Bear looks like my neighbor's cat,
Or is it a duck? Let's ponder that.

Dreams of stardust whisper my name,
But can they help at this silly game?
Constellations wink, full of spark,
As I trip on starlight in the dark.

My fingers stretch towards a moonbeam,
But life's no fairy tale or sweet dream.
In the vastness, we twist and twirl,
For questions orbit, as stardust unfurl.

The Horizon of Hope

In a world that's so unclear,
We search for signs, perhaps a deer.
Funny faces in the clouds,
We giggle low, we laugh out loud.

Questions dance in baffled minds,
While quirky memes are what one finds.
Pondering how cats might rule,
We fill the dark with our own fuel.

A fortune cookie whispered right,
Said fortune's gone, it took a flight.
Yet amid the riddles and the jest,
Our humor keeps us feeling blessed.

So let us toast to all that's vague,
With a rubber chicken, what a gag!
For life may seem a twisted jest,
But laughter truly is the best.

Embracing the Ambiguity

Lost in thoughts that seem bizarre,
Are aliens here, or near a bar?
We scratch our heads, sip coffee slow,
With socks that clash in bright rainbow.

Maps lead us where we do not know,
A journey meant for a show or two.
Pin the tail on the donkey's fate,
What a ride, oh wouldn't it be great?

Jokes between the folds of time,
Muddled lines in rhythm and rhyme.
Once a genie had a flare,
But in the bottle, he found despair.

Yet in this haze of fun-filled doubts,
Kindred spirits cling, no droughts.
Let's dance on toes where logic ends,
In a world where laughter never bends.

The Unfolding Enigma

What's the riddle, who's the sage?
Open a book, turn the page.
Chased a tail of a playful tease,
Caught it once, now it's a breeze.

A traffic stop for silly thoughts,
With a licorice twist, life's tauts.
Why do ducks march in a line?
Are their secrets more divine?

With each mishap and silly joke,
We sprinkle laughter, pass the smoke.
Life's a party, quite absurd,
Filled with nonsensical words unheard.

An unfolding tale of twists and fun,
It's just begun, and we've not run.
With a wink, let's cheers to whimsy,
In this cosmic dance, so flimsy.

In the Absence of Closure

Questions swirl like autumn leaves,
In a dance, the mind deceives.
Wandering thoughts, oh what a mess,
Like a cat that lost its press.

Final notes without a chord,
In this game, it's never bored.
We find delight in open trails,
As humor paves where logic fails.

Navigating through the haze,
Embrace the fog in witty ways.
Potatoes dressed for some fine dining,
Oh life, your humor's so defining.

Here we stand in moments grand,
Holding dreams and comic plans.
In the gaps, we laugh the most,
In the absence, we raise a toast.

When Will the Veil Lift?

Why do socks always disappear?
The laundry monster is near,
It munches, it crunches, it's sneaky,
And leaves the world feeling geeky.

Questions swirl in a merry dance,
Why did I wear these pants by chance?
The popcorn's gone, but where's the fun?
Oh look, a cat! Is she the one?

We ponder the mysteries galore,
Like why do we trip over the floor?
Perhaps the answer's just out of sight,
Behind the fridge, chilling with delight.

So let's toss our doubts to the breeze,
And search for giggles to tease,
For life's too quirky to take too deep,
Let's laugh out loud and forget to sleep!

The Unfinished Symphony

I wrote a tune on a napkin,
With ketchup stains as my captain,
The notes are stuck in my head like glue,
And my cat thinks it's all for her too.

Each chord's a jigsaw, scattered apart,
With missing pieces straight from the heart,
I hum as I juggle my coffee cup,
And wonder if it's time to give up.

Beethoven would scoff at my style,
But what if I just grin and reconcile?
A symphony of chaos and nail polish,
Should have a concert for all to demolish.

So here I stand, with my batty sounds,
Awaiting the praise that never surrounds,
For every mix-up is part of the plan—
An unfinished tune played by an unfinished man.

Seeking the Light in the Abyss

Down in the depths of the fluffy gray,
I searched for wisdom's bright buffet,
But all I found was a rubber duck,
Which quacked at me with a tone of luck.

I peered into shadows, what did I see?
A sock puppet challenging me to a spree,
"Join me in chaos, let's stir up some fun!"
And suddenly searching didn't feel like a run.

The abyss giggled with every blunder,
As I stepped through puddles of wacky wonder,
The light? Oh yes, I think I've got it,
It's just a glow from a fridge that won't quit.

So let's embrace this absurd parade,
Where questions dissolve like a truth charade,
And laughter fills the dark like confetti,
What were the answers? I guess we're not ready!

Reflections on a Blank Canvas

A canvas waits with a hopeful stare,
I ponder ideas that float in the air,
But all I find is a brush with no paint,
And a cactus that thinks it's a saint.

I splatter some thoughts that don't mix well,
The colors greet me with a cheerful yell,
"Let's make a masterpiece, add some flair!"
Only to find that it's just thin air.

With every stroke, I giggle and sigh,
Like Picasso on a rollercoaster high,
Each mark is a riddle, a jumbled scheme,
What if life's just one big color scream?

So here's to the chaos, the mess we create,
As we doodle our dreams on life's empty plate,
With laughter our guide, may we paint with glee,
For a laugh is the liveliest brush there can be!

Waves of Unfound Clarity

A jellyfish floated, quite profound,
Chasing answers it never found.
Tides tease the truth, then swiftly go,
Splashing wisdom in a frothy show.

Seagulls squawk tales of the deep,
While crabs dance on, lost in sleep.
The ocean giggles at questions asked,
A riddle wrapped in a wave, so masked.

In every swell, confusion churns,
But who needs answers when a tide turns?
We surf on doubt, in sunny bliss,
Grinning wide, as we reminisce.

So ride the crest, don't miss the fun,
Embrace the waves, leave answers undone.
Life's a beach, with sand in toes,
And laughter echoes where certainty goes.

The Horizon of Possibilities

Look past the edge, where sky meets sea,
Is that a clue or just a tree?
With binoculars made of dreams and hope,
We search for signs on a wobbly slope.

A hot air balloon, it drifts away,
Chasing rainbows, in bright display.
What's beyond that horizon line?
Perhaps a café serving good red wine?

Or maybe just clouds playing hide and seek,
With whispers of wisdom, quite unique.
Every sunset, a colorful tease,
We giggle at fate, and simply freeze.

Future's a puzzle, scattered on sand,
A jester's game played by fate's hand.
So let's toast to chances that come our way,
Isn't life grand? Let's laugh and play.

Conversations With Silence

In the room of quiet, giggles abound,
Where silence shouts without a sound.
Whispers of thoughts, they dance and prance,
As we ponder deep in a staring glance.

What did you say? Oh, never mind,
The thoughts we chase are hard to find.
A riddle here and a joke over there,
Silence grins, with mystery to share.

Cup of tea cooling on a shelf,
It seems the silence talks to itself.
It winks and nods like a wise old sage,
While we scribble nonsense on a blank page.

So let's toast our cups to all the unspoke,
And laugh at the thoughts that have gone up in smoke.
For in this stillness, we find our cheer,
The best of friends, when the end is near.

Illusions of Definitive Truths

A wizard declared with a spark of flair,
"Truth is easy, just look over there!"
But when I turned, nothing was found,
Just a squirrel dancing around the ground.

With stars in jars and moons on strings,
We craft our tales of peculiar things.
Each certainty crumbles like cake on a plate,
Leaving crumbs of confusion that soon accumulate.

A fortune cookie cracked, with words so sly,
"Find the truth, but don't ask why!"
With laughter we scrawl on the backs of our hands,
Making plans for lives that nobody understands.

So chase the tiny, elusive glow,
And tickle the fates with a hearty throw.
For in this circus of all that's absurd,
We've learned to dance with the silence unheard.